BETWEEN SO MANY W

# Between So Many Words

*Poems*

RIC HOOL

RED SQUIRREL PRESS

First published in the UK in 2016 by Red Squirrel Press
www.redsquirrelpress.com

Designed and typeset by Gerry Cambridge

Cover photograph *Y twig, O acorn cup, Q shell* by Colin Burt
Interior scraperboard vignettes by Tim Rossiter
Copyright © Ric Hool 2016

A CIP catalogue record is available from the British Library.

ISBN: 978 1 910437 31 5

Printed in the UK by Martins the Printers using acid-free
paper sourced from mills with FSC chain of custody
certification.
www.martins-the-printers.co.uk

FSC
www.fsc.org
MIX
Paper from
responsible sources
FSC® C004309

# Contents

*This collection is dedicated to Lyla*
*&*
*in memory of Anne Cluysenaar and Lee Harwood*

## A Blue Day

So many intensities of blue,
the colour migrates
into a chorus of shades
appearing and fading,
tints refining themselves
like the memory of Atlantis
arriving out of books
over horizons of time.

Distances of blue reach out.
Oceans and untouchable
skies mirror each other's depth
sending the eye to uncertainty,
dispatching sight to magic
and mind to imagination as blue
tones birth at 450 and leak out
at 490 nanometre wavelengths
rolling into the day.

# The Kingdom of Ends

You go to the heart
where laws indwell
on this warm February day.

Violin, piano and cello
remain in your head; the sun
posts itself between horizontal blinds.

Light ladders the table, each rung
climbed with conversation, until
a snake slides words back down.

Nothing appears to be plain.
Meaning, a satellite in orbit,
sometimes close then far off.

Air is a soup of light-caught motes
hardly heavy enough to land,
swept into currents by a busy waitress.

This is the heart and this is the law
pounding away in a long-lit room
towards a journey's end.

# A Geography of Words

About then, above thought,
across mind's river after flood
—against that flow, along new banks
amidst jettisoned waste,
we hid.

Around nightfall, at that time
before coldness, behind each other,
we walked below broken branches,
between torn trees beyond water's threat,
into darkness.

Underneath emotion, over consequences,
on past reason, until early morning's dead chill,
till thinnest sunlight laid greyness
upon rickety stiles.

There, surrounded by newness
and choked soakaways, beside reeds
nerved by winds, the sky began
over a world wrecked with words.

# The Rabbit & The Hat

Tide shapes a new relationship with land
on the early morning beach at Llanfairfechan.

Looking across the Menai Strait, the peep-peep
of an oystercatcher deepens desertion.

There is the smell of time. A time embedded
in my arm bones and knuckles of my fist.

It's there in a hand axe where craft and
skill pushed labour to ceremony.

Spirit and implement become indivisible,
the axe a key to another place.

This sand, that sea, those mountains so near,
so many identities depleting and discovering themselves.

Later, towards evening, a sunset burnishes sand
and turns sea to armour.

Air-shimmers warp moments.

# Broadcast

Today's radio news was interesting.
A man signed up his corpse
for mummification - somehow
seeding himself to the cosmos
as liquids slowly give up his body
leaving it desert dry over which
scientific whispers will be
atmospheric threats.

Gaddafi's Libya is shrinking, days away
from eclipse, as particles of time head
south over sands. The liberating army
must be tired: gunfire replaces Berber languages.

There, bodies dispatch their liquids without celebrity.
The leaden word of radio is god in the ear
drawing this listener nearer and nearer to a far-away tale.

# A Game for Wittgenstein

Language leaves its bruise.

Lindisfarne, that tidal outpost
blown off Northumberland's mainland
joined by tread-way, witnessed monks
mark *The Godspells*. Those words
seen as light and felt as heat, radiate
from page to brand the mind.

I carry the cross of one
who abandoned the cradle
to nose out but now returns to hearth.
That place of ignition.

Sky sweeps overhead and land
pushes up on my soles—I tread
in the footstep of language
bringing tongue toward the indefinite.

## Why We Use Language

There is something
in the word, waterfall…
That one, two, three
trinity of sound that moves
beyond letters, beyond but
held in spelling,  the spell.
The fall of water
as it breaks from its bed
to lose itself to be
shattered by light,
as it leaps air.

There is something
in a word towards reality.

# More light! Give me more light!

Early morning January, early
enough for light to be vague, for
darkness to be gloom. There is
little movement. Right now
it's me burrowing

into something unborn.
This earliest of months a bridge
between a thing forgotten and that
about to happen—an illness
incubated and primed.

A heron's outline is poorly etched.
It lands, turning ninety degrees
at the last to stand statue,
dagger beak poised to strike.

Slowly grey surrenders. Sunlight creeps
commando over bones of vegetation.
Such persistent archaeology.

## Lave

At low tide they are markers in the estuary
occupying the same spot as forefathers,
a dwindle of lave netmen searching the surface for signs,
a bubble, a purr of water pushed by a fin.

Waist deep in danger, they know the river
and work with it. Spread rimes are outstretched
arms embracing the water's run which tensions
the net, bellowing it into a yawn.

Fingers sense the net filaments in spider-like waiting,
one twitch enough to trigger the ambush.
A man steps back, raising the rock staff in front
springing the lave net above writhed in silver trophy.

Lave is to wash, perhaps to feel
the wash of time in The Severn curdling
with the sea, its undertow of secrets bumping
and flattening neoprene waders against legs.

*See note i*

# Putcher

Grips drain the spains into reens, slow moving
in summer or stagnant against stanks which keep the water
high enough for livestock to drink, for dragonflies
to rise imago, to wing, navigating the ditches.

It is easy to dream the Caldicot Levels in the slow
drone of warm months, cow pat-buzzed and swooped with swifts,
harder to consider the blocked and frozen gouts of winter
scythed by bitter winds funnelled up The Bristol Channel.

The local mind down centuries attuned to water, its
rise and fall twice daily a steady heartbeat, bleeding
the land of it at low tide and preventing inundation at high,
catching the rhythms between calm and storm.

To live off land and, from May to half August, off water
was the way. Hecks, crucks, cribs and here called putchers,
baskets set in ranks ready to trap thew salmon striking
upriver along ingrained lines of origin to milt and spawn.

To prepare then for the first day of May, split hazel rods
and plait with autumn-cut withy. Old men and young
together in story, hazel and willow. Every finished putch
must last two seasons—a third with repair.

 With gape end open to tide, the conical traps are fixed, some
to flood ranks, some to ebb ranks, ready to swallow bounty.
The putcher fishermen linger like last turnstones, eyes keen
on the return run as mud banks and traps rise from the river.

*See note ii*

## Towards Sleep

In bed listening to the world emptying.
Eyes stare at a ceiling, gazing through
disordered thoughts that are boundaries of being.

How high from which a fall is caught.
It moves Titanic towards its iceberg.

Room temperature drops and covers pulled up
against sleep's jury. Weather attacks windows.
History & future an undergrowth of restlessness.

## Clean Living Under Difficult Circumstances

It's difficult.
I want to slip
my hand in yours,
empty and loose
as you walk beside me.
It's difficult,
looking at a bead of sauce
on the corner of your lips
and not lick it away.
It's difficult
because, for sure,
I'd move from there
to a kiss, to embrace, to…
It's difficult
being cool around you
when a shock wave,
crashes through, wanting
to take you. It's difficult
sitting opposite whilst you drink
tea, all seems commonplace,
ordinary, as if we are somewhere
far from Llandudno.
It's difficult looking out to the Menai Strait,
so great, so lonely, yet
shining like opportunity. Then
the sun goes down. The sea
growls, going this way and that.
It's difficult
not putting cards on the table
already set
with strict napkins and cutlery.
It's difficult saying things not wanting to say,
the tongue hitting the wrong bumpers,
the pinball swallowed.

It's difficult
looking into your eyes
without coming closer.
It's difficult
hiking a mountain without you,
each breath goes out
to nothing but your being
there, and the air is
honey in the mind
taking the moment
to wherever you are.
It's difficult.
It's difficult. It's
getting harder to say,
and dreams remain
their selfish selves
washed up inside eyelids
broken from sleep.
Hearing you speak,
eating each word, that's how
I become a foxgloved bee.
It's difficult,
I brush past, get hooked
by cleavers of your perfume.

There's a bomb,
a machine gun ready to blow,
shrapnel about to sing through air.
There is…
And then…
How will…?

It's difficult
raking shorelines,

the horrors that lie
beneath seaweed, or
skimming a pebble like hope
counting each staggered bounce—it
ultimately sinks.
It's difficult
reading the glyphs
with blind fingertips, having faith
in truth, illusions, someone said,
we have forgotten
are illusions – as if that helps
or makes a steadier world.
Learning to speak,
learning to fight,
to write a near-missed thought,
to map it all out…
attempting 'clean living
under difficult circumstances',
it's difficult.

*'Clean living under difficult circumstances': Pete Meadon's definition*
*of Mod Philosophy*

# La Gomera Poems

# Independence Day

*A La Gomera poem*

The ferry heaves away, churning
a foam umbilical cord that winds behind.
A stump of rainbow reaches up
as sunlight catches spray and follows.
There is the smell of engines, a sense of power
felt through the feet.

If I were to fall would this be love's landscape,
a succession of toing and froing for crumbs of intimacy;
a wallet of tickets from there to here, from here to there
kept as mementos, as if love needs such things?
Timetables, rough seas, cancelled crossings,
the emptiness of squalid waiting rooms
all have their part to play.

To find every unknown self involves so many
terrains, so many climates, so many expeditions, it's difficult
to know how to prepare or how well equipped a person is
to deal with the wandering—the wondering, and being
locked inside and out, like it is when a language is missing.
And why is the man opposite sharpening a knife?

The island recedes into blueness, shrinking
the white houses on its hillsides until they appear
strung like a series of necklaces mimicking clouds
about to lasso the highest peaks.

*See note iii*

# A Private Ownership of Feeling

*A La Gomera poem*

In a place of simple ways
all attends to life,
each moment to the next
without artifice.
Ice melts as air moves
as hearts beat as words search
as people work whilst fish swim.

Pigeons are winged chariots
circling an arena of air
again and again, once more, each
time one drops out.
The race is forgotten as past is
mislaid as wings close,
                 finished books.

There is rhythm,
a drift of people.
Colours curdle
as whispers purr
as time suspires.

Another kit of pigeons stir the sky.

# The Love of a Public Road

*A La Gomera poem*


Men and women on the bus could be anything
from sixty to one hundred and sixty years
in age and talk loudly across aisles.

There is energy and a last meal strong with garlic
oiling every breath. The journey becomes a feast
winding thousands of feet, bends hardly able
to take the motor's length.

The bus system shrinks the island in cheap fares
and easy drivers who stop on request. A woman
steps down, then steps through the threshold of her front door.

There is a central idea extending from the kitchen out,
by whatever means, and back, which sustains. It is
not just food but the prattle of everyday happenings
that nourish these people, sure as transfusion,
from the coastline inward; from the island's heart out.

# We are Participatory Beings

*A La Gomera poem*

Misguided rockets arrive too early
scoring long furrows of concern
before detonating sprays of radiance
upon an unready sky, only accumulating darkness.

Fireworks over the sea double the effect
throwing back lightning echoes.
Distress or celebration?  Here lies
a twist to a poem of mistaken gestures.

On the mountain rising sheer from the harbour
is a beacon near a statue.
The statue is of Christ. The light
guides ships in to safety.

Somehow knowledge of the statue, it
being there, is profound. In the dark
looking up from lower ground its profile
is blacker than the heavens it leans upon.

# Thought as a River Through Air

*A La Gomera poem*


Midnight cars down the mountain
are fireflies burning against darkness
swinging to the score of their own
invisible music held within a solar system
membrane of windscreen and windows.

Tired lovers lean in to each other not saying
much, listening to the low tones of radio,
tyres and engine composing; hearing what they think
is silence easing them down to the small town
itself near but not yet asleep. They permit me

to join them, these deep-drinking dreamers, and
allow me to imagine with them along alleys
and backstreets that criss-cross the mind
making so many corners of tiredness, making
thinking as much a travelling as a construction.

The trickle of travellers dries to an intermittent flicker.
Occasional headlights splash yellow magnets ahead.

# Morning Song of the Island

A La Gomera poem

Suitcase wheels singing
down the ramp, singing
busy boat horns singing
shake the seafront.

Lined up taxis singing
air conditioning singing
engines purring, singing
'Come, I take you!'

Cups of coffee singing
roast aroma singing
'Wakey-wakey!' singing
be alive.

Harbour fish singing
at the surface singing
'Have you bread?' singing
'Bread for song?'

The island song singing
open arms singing
sun-ignited sea sings
the island morning song.

# Willingness for Realization

I am witness to made things that want me
to believe they are real:
                                plastic roses.
Their coloured petals arrive as red.

The roses have been put in a glass vase
through which I see. There is
water half way up the vase.

                        The water
alters perception further. Magnified
green plastic stems are dislocated
from those above the surface.

I look away then back. All is
as it should be:
a vase of red roses needing a little more water.

# From Nowhere Arrive

Helpless and ignorant
in attempt to work into words,
raw experience and turn it
like lathed wood to something
I say is mine.

Utterance comes dumb to the tongue
and letters desert each other
like woodlice from under a lifted stone.

Towards outposts to win their possibility,
I am charmed and bound by spells
                    —a would-be caster.
Charming and spelling, both
acts of transformation.

From nowhere arrive:
        *'Mr Watson, come here…'*

*'What hath God wrought?'*

                *'That's a small step for man…'*

                        *'lo'*

*See note iv*

# Sketches of an Artist

*A poem sequence dedicated to art deco artist,
Tamara De Lempicka*

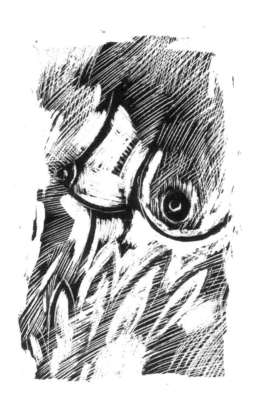

## Tamara 1

A room of paintings becomes
your world. The silent voice of gesture
as light catches horizons of foreheads
and redness of cruel mouths—they are soundless
too, below eyes filled with secrets.

Such flawless bodies—almost
statues in two dimensions, alabaster breasts
seek no hiding, your brushstrokes
swell them. A group

of four nudes twined and knotted
like clematis, want to burst
the quadrant of canvass, to live
wildly outside its keeping.

## Tamara 2

Cocaine disorders time, so nights become
a succession of wanderings to game with
women and sailors, reeling from one
outrage to the next. Dancing
groin-grinding into corners, never
giving or taking a kiss, those red petals
later for canvass. First gesso,
the preparation on which
all depends. Here ideas are arms
hung over a lover's shoulders,
a stockinged leg whispered by a hand
and eyes bright with otherness.

## Tamara 3

The myth is not
through art but in its making—models
open to the world but you do not
free yourself from the object
and continue to describe it
by definite boundaries,
matching a life of attachments
played out like radio dramas:
a lot packed in. Single figures
fill canvasses, large
as they are in life, brief
as they are in life, bold
as they are in life.

# Tamara 4

Rafaela disrobes, enters,
a mist of chiffon drifts from shoulder to hip,
raises an arm across her eyes
in protection: the light.
Her body in use once more, but gentler...no
rough hands demand money's worth
or breath, fetid, hot and fast.
Instead, stillness is mandate, she holds
a frozen moment that is captured
in the nearby sound of brush
upon the memory of canvass.

*See note v*

## Tamara 5

After the fires for years
confined within you, controlled,
curtailed in breaks and hacked-out
emotional undergrowth,
a spark leaps over the safety
area. A small notion
arced in exploration
as if it was always
meant to happen. It lands.
Something new is on offer
a different world ignites,
fanned by fresh winds.

## Tamara 6

Café life, its constant call, not easy
to fit when pleasure creeps in
small hours of morning
and daylight demands painting.
Another name to add to the list
thinking Art is freedom's key. Kizette
models again and again, is
all but painted out of life, is
left drying on an easel, hanging
on a wall, on show
in a gallery, staring out
searching for a mother who,
staking her claim in America, writes,
*There will be no Christmas together this year.*

*See note vi*

## Tamara 7

Burnt hats of retribution keep Tamara
from the old country and in a new world
pioneering her art. She finds lost
acquaintances, a raggle-taggle
European aristocracy washed up
on rocket-shaped buildings of modernism.

## Tamara 8

Tamara talks grand dukes,
she is Baroness Kuffner, continues,
King Alphonse XIII,
princes, poet-playboy Gabriel
D'Annunzio, Mussolini
—a repertoire of cobwebbed aristocracy
from war-changed Europe.
Ever fearful of anything
other than wealth, she does not grasp
how she squanders her place in art
by her covenant with pleasure.

*See note vii*

## Tamara 9

The sensation of wood splitting, that
moment strength gives…what happens
is detail not as was first obvious.
Revealed fibres are complex
currents of youth, vigour once pliant,
hardened over years. Tamara rests
her high resolution signature brushwork
for impressionist palette knives
putting youth away.

## Tamara 10

Bored, chain smoking, your brand,
tipped, long and dangled
between naked and heavily ringed fingers,
discomforted by age; its nursed thoughts.
The Paris studio closed, a ghost
collection stored in Houston, the final
pickings. You inhale, stub them out
half-finished like thoughts moving by
half-remembered importance.
The room is fugged by white bodies
expiring in ashtrays.

## Tamara 11

Your volcanic life
complete is returned
to magma, to Mount Popo.

Uncertain winds that day,
blow your ashes back
into the faces of those watching.

*See note viii*

# Running Away with the Hairdresser

The town is a wedge between them
cleaving their joined minds. His wants
to forget, hers to remember…
The Station Hotel between the open legs of
Light Street and Shady Street, already glowing
at 4 pm with transformation, absorbs steady custom.

He surges from purposelessness.
Eyes closed, he turns his back on the place,
its reason misshaped as its buildings
and shakes his cloddish feet into running,
hauling her behind.

She falters, divided, sure as a corner splits
the way. Her shoes think for themselves,
heels digging the road chipping in arrest.
Linked hands rupture like a broken bicycle chain,
they each move at unregulated speeds of intent.

*See note ix*

# The New Revenge of Rain-in-the-Face

Rain and the beat goes on. Goes on in drummed rhythms
variant on surfaces. Rain, punching out of skies grey and low
over mountains. Rain sliding down window panes, choking drains,
bending a man double as he walks into it, straining
his body towards home. Rain, Noah-like, you get the picture?

Rain transforming fields to ponds, turning car tyres
angrily through puddles spraying fantastic fountains
over pavements . Squelching wellington boot-weather rain,
sodden jeans below water proof jacket rain.
Rain that leaves you careless of keeping dry,

stings the eye, mascara-running 1950s,
*I'll do My Crying in the Rain* rain.
Hood up, eyes down, pavement bingo, no one talking
till they get indoors. Rain that's a river with holes.
Rain that is tigers and wolves.

Car headlight-caught rain makes the night right
for espionage—an agent in each upturned collar.
Flood alert rain rising in sandbag eyes, everything upstairs,
where's the insurance policy rain. First volley
to last salvo fired from dreadnought cloud-cruised skies.

# From Africa, Out

Tropos,
      a turn, twists away, its force
a tornado: the brickwork comes apart.

        From ruin we go
          forward

into space in fashion of Northern Lights
or stars burning bright across eye-caught skies.

Always the Men Morris of Misrule
untie the dance, unstring its tune
to filch from the hat to thirst
                    at drinkless bars.

In poem, in picture
by a stream, his body hacked,
fallen from the charts,
from boogie-woogie popped dreams
Pindar hears Orpheus scream the blues,
'Hell grants what love seeks'
reverberated in empty rock n roll wardrobes.

It spirals to now and on…

              'C'mon baby, let's do the twist.'

*'C'mon baby, let's do the twist.'*
*from Chubby Checker's 1962 hit, 'The Twist'*

# Eleven Views of a Secret

*A poem sequence dedicated to jazz bass phenomenon Jaco Pastorius*
*'The world's greatest bass player'.*

*See note x*

# Jaco 1 (Intro)

You are spring blossom
        —newness. Feel yourself
                burst!

## Jaco 2

Empty African drums hollow the soul
and morning sky melts night
to shine a rocket shot from Cape Canaveral.

A 'Portrait of Tracy' hangs delicately
and slightly askew on its bright nail,
rumbled by low frequency sound waves.

*See note xi*

# Jaco 3

Music's bright light beams
and picks out fleet-footed waves
from crest to crest.

'(Used To Be A) Cha-Cha'
 its relentless rhythm
exits the short distance,
Cuba to Florida.

*See note xii*

## Jaco 4

Pastorius, unlike a shepherd,
scatters notes over a score,
opening music's pen, exploding
captives to the landscape,
the escape-scape, colours mixing
then resting in fusion.

## Jaco 5

Having taken the frets out
you slide notes into something
that compliments the second sweep
of a Rolex wristwatch.

## Jaco 6

Two seams of gold
stitching denim jeans:
your playing and not.

That fabric too workmanlike
and running stitch
unimaginative.

          But then
there's the tightness,
the inseparable strength.

## Jaco 7

Taking back the unwanted kiss
—all belongs to a generation that has been
destroyed and made again, fabulous.

This is the beginning of myth.
But you wait in the limbo of legend.
How long before you are remade an Orpheus?

The speech of your four stringed instrument
breaches musical convention. For the likes
of you, trees gain their souls;
                              lose their wood.

## Jaco 8

Living between so many words, I wonder,
'On what terms do you enter my world?'

You are felt like the flight path of a swift
through my body. An osmic recollection

making a circumstance suddenly form.
A re-visitation to somewhere known

before consciousness—a well-kept dream;
an infrasonic sensation scorched by purple flares.

## Jaco 9

It works by cogs, huge,
with bone-crunching teeth
revolved by industrious smaller ones
spinning quicker, in turn
spun by a diamond,
never musically worn down.

## Jaco 10

It's late and the party winds down
past messed-up tables
spilt with drink and tiredness
blinked in eyes so bright
only hours of music ago. The name
Jaco, heavy like the smoke-hung air
doesn't leave easily.

Six days after the brawl took away
his high cheek bones, the last
composition in his head, bled,    burst.

# Jaco 11 (Outro)

Raspberry-sweet from the bush
soft fruit, summer-swollen
beneath swallows and swifts, time is
borrowed, held in a spell
of ignited harmonics.

Together, you and those
bright notes, all too brief.

## December: Remote

Streams clatter down
clowning their way through each season
below ash, oak, sycamore smoke
from Glynmercher's chimney.

The drive down throws up a jay—that road
a trick of twists and delinquent cambers.

Geography is deep; is everywhere.
Strata and correspondence are substances of imagining.
They say. They are.
Nothing residual but the future.

Over the bridge, under hawthorn, across
two fields and jumped freshets to a gate,
to a door. This way a person arrives.

Clothes never change him.
There is no colour in them that is
not his colour, that is
not his light.

I sing his life,
not counting steps
but know that many
have been taken.

*See note xiii*

# Stoned

At Scorehill Stone Circle
summer evening light
casts aside common experience
in the way digging makes a find.

Granulations.
Glinted specks of lustre
return borrowed sun.

The assembled stones
changed to something celestial.
An inhalation of time.

# Long-Term Investment

The beach east of Charmouth,
a wobbly line of memory,
throws up imprints of time.

Each mud slide surrenders
long-held secrets—more exclusive
than any Swiss bank account.

## Arriving at Discovery Arriving

A cliff route over an ancient sea floor of shell-rock
throws out fingers, promontories, some cut
to sea stacks and mined by caves.
The Atlantic pushes in.

Down the steep cliff towards sea, a café squats
beside a blow-hole in a cup of red rock.
The menu is fish.

Men with spears rise and fall in sea-swells.
They dive deeply, lost for minutes
before the surface is disturbed,
broken by gasps. They haul themselves
ashore fixing their bodies on rocks.

The swim of light covers time.
Waves buckle towards day's end.

At that closure, hot Sahara arrives, a wandering tribe
advancing evening to spiced darkness
as air from Africa whispers its sleepless night,
carrying the whimper of jackals, perhaps,
sparks of Berber campfires.

Eyes and stars are awake.
They shine out to each other.
A box lined with mirrors.

# The Dreamer

As distant and as close
at any time in sleep
they come, sometimes
as succulent jellyfish
pulsing in oceans; sometimes
as a hard-hooved stampede;
sometimes as a finger-wagged warning.

However they arrive, they arrive
and startle like stepping too deeply
off a curb or biting too hard on a wafer.

They are a life within a life.
I wake to their treasure.

## Uncertainty of Time

Without sails the masts arrive as spikes
out of water. The barque, 'Belem', comes
in late afternoon sea-haze to anchor
just off shore. It twists time
with its silent presence. All evening,
all night, not near nor far, a distance
called 'offing'. The darkness between
this house and ship is punctured by exchanges
of lights as rooms here, cabins there,
are entered and left, simulating a code
preceding trafficked contraband, perhaps
conducting something played out in another century.

# Thirteen Notes to Juliet

*1*

When attracted never look away.
Let the image amplify.
Juliet it is you.

*2*

Mirrored on the surface of burgundy,
you are blushed in its colour; your lips
move in mute conversation.

*3*

A balcony, your hair
dangled in a fairy tale
that draws a lover,
hand after hand,
to your presence.

*4*

Love is loneliness,
it worries itself, lost
in slippery moments.

*5*

Juliet,
your hair curls, the wind
winds it into whispers.

6

The first rule of writing:
never give up on obsession.

Juliet,
forming each word forges links
in the sturdiest chain; daybreak
brings no lightness.

Juliet,
it is breakfast but words
do nothing but feed hunger.
Love is starvation.

7

The orchards are picked
roughly but joyously, sweetness
pressed for autumn merriment.
Juliet,
you are summer's effervescence.

8

To run, mad with your name,
repeat it again, again, cupping
its sound to catch its echo.
You are not trapped this way.

*9*

As day lengthens into warm evening
and street café tables gurgle in conversation,
this pen writes with its own mind,
shaping thoughts like winged creatures

set free.

*10*

Looking far out to the universe
the same as looking far into ourselves:
light gains intensity in darkness.

*11*

Butterfly days turn
to mothy nights.

*12*

Juliet,
the ghost of you
makes *being* a spectre.
The shoe is on the other foot
as the hollow man shambles
along the hollow road.

*13*

In this chamber of language
sleep purrs, breathing slows
and Juliet carries her candle
forever on Escher's staircase.

# Chiaroscuro

Attending an organ recital
in a church. I begin your picture.

Music soothes mind into rushless rhythm.
Like drawing a bucket from a deep well
slowly you become more than outline.

Roughening paper with graphite,
whispering darkness over its surface
scratching away the day until evening
reveals an image of you.

# Vogue La Galère

*'Row the galley'*
> *Let the world go how it will: let us keep on whatever happens*

Tomorrow is set aside, that is
it is designated for something
unexpected. Perhaps a walk
to an abandoned village
stumped in dilapidation and fallen roofs?

Tomorrow is earmarked.
A saunter around dreary streets
observed by dodgy shop windows
clung amber with film,
advertising out-of-date jars.

Tomorrow is tagged.
An arrangement made before signs
swung the wrong way, before the world
cooled and doors bolted.

# Rooming-House

The corridor, bled by rooms,
has doors opening and closing,
                opening and closing.

Hinges and handles almost soundless,
occupants peeping out then returning.
                An orchestration of heads.

History has no past; memory no need.

A door gently opened
is never slammed shut.
The key that unwinds its lock
kept in deepest, safest, emotion.

# Then—Now—Later

July borrowed from June
the once boggy track is charity dry
but out of habit the way is skirted
to avoid sinking—it's an effort
of will to walk where I have not
since first discovering this ancient route.

On that day, wary of what was
unknown, the trail, no matter how claggy,
was a faithful leader urging steps forward.

Under todays flamed sky The Old Lady
of the Mountains, her grey shawl drawn
over her head is nowhere to be seen.
But she is here, somewhere, knitting
a misty future with webs of moisture.

Cast that veil she will… to begin another.
On that day to come I shall recall
this friendly one; insist it
burns a map of safe passage.

# Thirteen Friendships to Chris Torrance

# Thirteen Friendships to Chris Torrance

*1*

El Toro the bull
guarding its querencia
alert to a landscape of signals,

> sheep bustling along a path,
> the field gate's clink half a mile off,

put feet from slippers into outside shoes.

You make your stand
at Glynmercher Isaf
beneath a tree-broken sky
defended by streams on three sides
and feel land pick up the pulse of itself
> and world beyond.

*2*

It is December and winter weather
piles up either side of the track
the question to press on or go back?

A gift, my first on our first
Christmas of friendship must be delivered
and more snowfall confounds judgement.

Sheep are shadows of whiteness
stood quietly together
quizzing my presence.

You might not like whisky    it is
all the physical warmth I can offer
this quickly. The bottle
badly disguised, left, wrapped
and damp on your doorstep.

*3*

Paul Jones our glue on Thursday evening
until it changed. The emptiness
took getting used to.

Monday night too sudden
in the new-born week, senses
in recovery. Eventually

the playlist won. The blues
suckled our ears.
The geography between us, pioneered.

*4*

It's about soil

     standing on it

     digging it

     strata informing it

It's about soil

     how wet

     how dry

     how rain falls on it and when

It's about soil

     what's taken out

     what's put in

     its lightness

     its depth

     its warmth

It's about soil

     getting it under finger nails

     turning it with ached hands

     making it say *Shirley Poppy*

It's about soil

     and we call it poetry

*5*

The last Glynmercher bushman,
you dreamed Viv and brought her back
by evocation. She toppled
from a bucket moon to look
over your shoulder as you check
the max and min thermometer,
Old Moore's Almanac and mice damage
to early garden shoots. Tender ones
always need the greatest protection.

6

The day the goshawk came the sky showed
no sign of difference, a matt-grey
blanket of low stratus stretched
drumhead tight over the Nedd Fechan valley.

Springtime's hunger pushed the bird out,
its eyes fired-up for food and flight
stitched gaps large and small between
branches and trees, with precision.

Robert Creeley knew this trajectory, his
single eye worked for two, running
needle-narrow lines of sound
his hands outstretched and ready.

The day the goshawk arrived, static
clouds were zipped white by its courtship flight.
Perhaps your mind flew to Carshalton, to
impatient flesh danced in a skin-tight dress.

7

New moon, new weather:
a red fox, rod-straight brush,
out to taste twilight.

New moon's peel, lights
the owl-flown night, silent
                    —holy as a carol.

New moon caught
in darkness of your window
smiles back at itself.

New moon
        red fox
                carol
        a cottage window.

*8*

Hell in January after repeated rainstorms
silt the spring pipe, choking it.

A lightning strike shorts electrics
and wind picks up to test the slates.

Under siege it comes down to candles,
muddy tea and prayers to a roof god.

SAD, winter blues—call it what you like
it's as close as you get to giving up.

*9*

The weekly crusade to Cardiff
to adventure in creative writing—your
dawn chorus start from Glynmercher
to razzle-dazzle capital.

Bus changes coldly waited and timetabled
disappointment fought off, keeping yourself
from meeting an unwanted stare—you know
what it is to be a dove among hawks.

*10*

The envelope boldly written,
sellotaped for security, gloves
its letter bringing wildlife and weather
from the Upper Neath Valley.

Wind turbines have sprung up, thirteen
at last count, turning landscape space-rural
—tall, propeller-headed towers straight
out of a fifties sci-fi story.

Mice, slugs and snails had an after hours
garden party. Their noise stealthed
under the boom, boom, boom rave
at the countryside car park that throbbed
through an unslept night.

The mobile library service is axed!
Is this the way to promote reading?
Another thread tugged
from the frayed cloth of rural life!

The voice of activist resounds then mellows
into description of an evening sky,
buttercup-yellow light pencilling clouds
and there, the phrase, 'wheat-straw'.

*11*

We swapped curries
for cheese on toast
and spoke
of weather bombs
blue moons
and rode Rioja
with Don Quixote
winding across
La Mancha's high plains
tilting windmills along the way.


 Jet streaming on Jaco
past a red kite Valentine
whilst electric bars blacked out
bringing back a cold snap
  —'Never cast a clout'
a judicial blackcap chattered
and grabbing the ram by the horns
we dropped a cog and wound on
skidding tyres towards your birthday.

12

You want a hundred days
like today
     wired to sky
         watching swifts
              an Isla Negra on your lips
                   and butterfly-kissed hands

You want a hundred days
like today
     flowers bursting like bathers
         on a bank holiday beach
             horse show dreams
                —an ice-cream 99

You want a hundred days
like today
     remembering the girl
         you never could forget
             forgetting each tender hurt
                She was summer and its burning sun

Sitting on Peace Lawn
     poems and song
         flashing wheatears, bobbing wagtails
            Beltaine wide open
             the heat dribbles slowly on…

               you say you want a hundred days
               like today

*13*

We might be white saints with black minds
eavesdropping on whispers held in seasons,
radicles splitting from seed,
placing firm feet in soil
to blindly push pallid shoots
upward, urging them to break free,
to gasp air and rise high,
tumbling those numbers
Fibonacci threw
spiralling in leaf and flower and fruit
whilst roots ever-search deeper,
                              deeper,
                                    deeper.

# Ebbw Fach: Blaina

*February 2014*

The river swims one hundred yards off
winter-full and no sign of a dipper.
Everything on the river bed clings.

The valley is cut with song rising
from rough-throated water,
a drunkard singing itself homeward.

A sudden breeze scalps mist from the river
- air reclaiming its loan; twigs drop
a tick-tock of moisture.

Dampness holds a fox's night walk
strung in a necklace of musk.
It drives walked dogs jig jag to each scent post.

Sun is a promise behind grey curtains
- the day impatient for its presence.
A cockerel crows razor-throated.

Stroppy blackbirds cluck from shrubbery
knocking up heads of grazing sheep—disturbed
breakfast heavy in each stomach.

The river sweeps closer under a flimsy bridge
trapping flotsam into a makeshift dam.
A new song recorded: who writes them!

# The Great Invasion

*Winter storms 2013/2014*

They huddle around each other
unwanted children
orphaned
by a North American
polar vortex
quickly
running out of control
down a hill of pressure.

Wild changelings
pelted and growled
speedily
into vengeful packs
tooth and jowl
berserkers of enraged weather
splintering daylight
hammering night
against the bitten shield of coastline
challenging farmers
snapping their backs
fields left trembled in water.

They arrive with caveats:
*Storm Surge*
*Red Warning*
*Flood Alert*
*Risk to Life*
like fitting peaks
in an incurable illness.

And ropes are drawn taught
knotted and staked
and fear is a wire across the eye.

Without beginning or end
a uroboric machine self-perpetuates
making further claim on a blue planet.


There are islands on islands


Another day
rain ceases
sun shines.
That day a lifeboat
in the souls of the stricken.

Then rain starts again
churned out
by an Atlantic storm factory
a thousand miles west
where polar air presses
and breaks the skin
of sub-tropical warmth
to be carried in
a vagrant Jet Stream.


There grows a celebrity of weathermen.


Lost wetlands of sixty years gone
are terribly found so terribly found.
The drowned ground gurgles water from a dead mouth
and uncountable lifeless burrowers
inherit the earth.
Freshwater fish find solitude
in unknown submergences
—casting anglers have endless choice.

There is a newness brought to everything except history.
Bygone Januaries earmarked:
1362 'Grote Mandrenke' (The Great Drowning of Men)
1607 Tsunami (The Bristol Channel Floods)
1953 The North Sea Surge

Thousands dead.

Two reports from January 1953:
　　　Rabbits become sailors on the backs of swimming sheep
　　　until the bleating boats sink.
　　　No hands survive.

　　　Eyes looking out from Costa Hill Orkney
　　　are pressed into heads
　　　by 126 mile per hour winds.


January 2014 the wettest winter since 1767.


Soldiers bag sand against doors
　　　　—doorsteps like the Ghats at Varanasi.
A helicopter shudders air
it's downdraft planishing the water's surface.

Thinking is immediate
　　　　　　　　misery acute.
Cold hands shelter in damp pockets.
Everything familiar has fled—even a warm thought.
The high wall of heroism overshadows
the breaching of Mohne and Eder Dams.
In February 2014 acts of nature
are despised more than acts of war.

Over the Atlantic
a key winds the wind

tighter and tighter
the torque then
spins off another storm like a top.

This cyclone has fangs
and stampedes white-horsed waves
over open ocean
shoreward into corrals of sleeping fishing harbours.

This creature has the scent.
Too late its prey will wake
to howls and wet breath.


Water's make over
smooths land's pocked skin
and sky finds it face
on wet fields.

The language of plough
is unwritten on ground
and farm machines silenced
as parlance shrinks to locutions of wetness.

# Boot Hill

The Arctic Jet Stream sweeps too far south,
expectations change as rain
conditions each day, hollowing out ground,
enlarging  aquifers, priming them for collapse
during the dry Spring to come.

Elsewhere the tide to provide fresh drinking
water is out; famine floods in.
The occidental market, a house of cards,
senses frequent and stronger tremors.
Megalopolis hears air sucked up in its oil.
Lights are going out and who is in?

It's hot, getting hotter, paradoxically
cooler & getting colder. The corpse lies
with a gun in hand & bullet in heart.
Gunslingers get dropped one by one
but more come, and more come.
Common sense holds hands with Alice
as she dives down a rabbit hole.

Gunshots  ricochet off rainforest
puncturing the green lung whilst Gunmen
e-mail tallies to conglomerate accounts.

Chip is church, its congregation legion.
Common sense is somewhere as lights go out,
as screens go black as Alice blinks in the rabbit hole.

## Again and Once More

The white wall

The light

The scattering of moths

The deepening night

Knowing          how many times

                  of being

                        just here

# Notes

*i.* Lave net fishing is an old practice that has all but died out.
Single men stand in deep water, each with a large scoop-like net.
The lave net has a 'Y' shaped structure consisting of two arms
called *rimes* made from willow, which act as a frame from which the
net loosely hangs. This method of fishing was used in river estuaries
to catch salmon. The poem concerns the small group of lave net
fishermen still working out of Black Rock, Portskewett, on the
Welsh side of the River Severn estuary.

*ii.* Spelled *rhyne* in England and *reen* in Wales: a ditch. The reen
system on the Caldicot levels has the primary function of moving
water to sea from fields during the wettest months of the year, to
prevent flooding. *Grips* are small gullies which channel water to the
greater network of reens. Water levels are managed in the reens by
pens known as *stanks*, in which wooden planks can be set to raise the
water levels in summer and reduce them in winter.

Putcher fishing is a type of fishing (usually for salmon) which
employs a large number of putcher baskets, set in a fixed wooden
frame called a rank, against the tide in a river estuary.

*iii.* La Gomera is part of the Canary Islands. It is the second smallest
of the seven main islands of this group.

*iv.* 'Mr Watson, come here, I want to see you' was the first clear
message by telephone by Alexander Graham Bell on March 10, 1876.

'What hath God wrought?' was the first telegraph message
transmitted by Samuel F. B. Morse on 24th May 1844.

The first message on the ARPANET, the precursor of the Internet,
was sent on October 29, 1969. The message text was the word
'login'; the 'l' and the 'o' letters were transmitted but the system then
crashed. Hence, the literal first internet message was 'lo'.

*v.* Rafaela: a favourite model of Tamara De Lempicka.

*vi.* Kizette: daughter of Tamara De Lempicka.

*vii.* Tamara De Lempicka married her long-time patron and lover, Baron Raoul Kuffner, on 3 February 1934.

*viii.* Mount Popo: Tamara De Lempicka died March 18, 1980. Her ashes were scattered over the Mexican volcano Popocatepetl on 27 March 1980 by her friend Victor Manuel Contreras and her daughter Kizette.

*ix.* Running Away with the Hairdresser: painting by Kevin Sinnott (1995)

*x.* Jaco Pastorius: John Francis Anthony Pastorius III, born 1st December 1951 died 21st September 1987, was a hugely influential American jazz musician, composer and electric bass player. His playing style included intricate solos in the higher register which along with the 'singing' quality achieved on his fretless bass and his innovative use of harmonics changed the approach to playing the instrument. Jaco Pastorius died from injuries suffered from a fight with a nightclub bouncer.

*xi.* 'Portrait of Tracy': The title of a composition dedicated to Jaco's wife, Tracey Pastorius.

*xii.* '(Used To Be A) Cha-Cha': a composition by Jaco Pastorius.

*xiii.* Glynmercher: Glynmercher Isaf, poet Chris Torrance's remote cottage in the upper Neath Valley.

# Acknowledgements

'Sketches of an Artist' 1–4; 10 & 11 appeared in *Tears in the Fence* No. 56 Winter 2012/13.

'Independence Day' and 'Thought as a River Through Air' appeared in Envoi issue 163 November 2012.

'A Private Ownership of Feeling', 'We are Participatory Beings', 'The Love of a Public Road' and 'Connections Imagined after the Facts' appeared in *The Cannon's Mouth* issue 46 December 2012.

'The New Revenge of Rain-in-the-Face' appeared in *Poetry Wales,* issue 49.1 Summer 2013.

'December: Remote' and 'Boot Hill' appeared in *Scintilla* 17 (The Journal of the Vaughan Association) 2013.

'From Africa, Out' appeared in the *Double Bill* anthology (Red Squirrel Press, 2014).

'Thirteen Friendships to Chris Torrance' appeared in *Tears in the Fence,* No. 60 Autumn 2014

'Putcher' and 'Lave' appeared in the online poetry magazine *Molly Bloom*, January 2015.

'The Kingdom of Ends', 'A Geography of Words' and 'A Game for Wittgenstein' appeared in *Poetry Salzburg Review* 27, Spring 2015.

A NOTE ON THE TYPE

This volume is set in Bembo Book,
a contemporary reworking of the Renaissance
typeface Bembo, a type by Francesco Griffo used by
Aldus Manutius in 1495 to print
Cardinal Bembo's tract 'de Aetna'. The italic was based
on a design used in a publication produced in Venice
circa 1524 by the writing master, Giovantonio Tagliente.

Bembo Book has been designed to replicate the 'ink squash'
of the old hot metal Bembo, and to produce similar results
to those achieved from the hot metal version
when letterpress printed. It is a generally sturdier cut
than the original digital Bembo.